Name.................. Date..................

Write over the dotted letters and colour the picture.

Tom Tom Tom
Tom Tom Tom

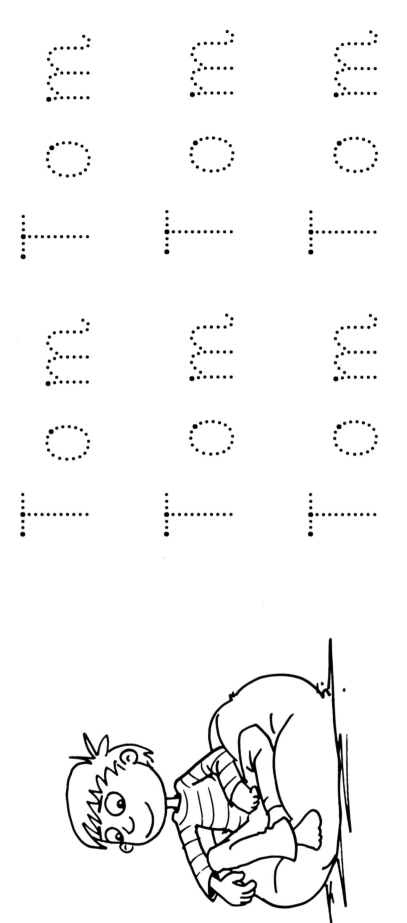

Write **Tom** on the dotted line by yourself.

....

Book 1 Activity 1

Handwriting activities from

Name.. Date..................

Write over the dotted letters and colour the picture.

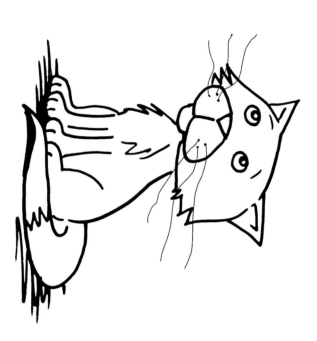

Write **cat** on the dotted line by yourself.

Name.......................... Date..........................

Write over the dotted letters and colour the picture.

Write **dog** on the dotted line by yourself.

Book 1 Activity 3

Handwriting activities from Jellly and Bean

Name.................................... Date....................................

Draw a line from each word to the correct picture.

Tom cat dog

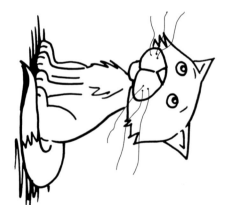

Write all three words by yourself on the dotted line.

....

Book 1 Activity 4

Handwriting activities from Jelly and Bean

Name.................................... Date....................

Draw a line from each phrase to the correct picture.

a cat on a dog

a dog on Tom

a cat on Tom

Write the words **on** and **a** on the dotted line.

....

Book 1 Activity 5

Handwriting activities from Jellly and Bean

Name.. Date..................................

Draw a line from each phrase to the correct picture.

| Tom **and** a dog |

| a cat **and** a dog |

| Tom **and** a cat |

Write the word **and** on the dotted line as many times as you can.

....

Book 1 Activity 6

Handwriting activities from Jelly and Bean

Name........................ Date........................

Write over the dotted letters and colour the picture.

Write **big dog** on the dotted line by yourself.

Book 2 Activity 1 — Handwriting activities from Jellly and Bean

Name.. Date....................

Draw a line from each phrase to the correct picture.

fat cats

Write **a** or **i** in the correct places in the words below.

big tin

f_t   c_ts   b_g   t_n

Book 2 Activity 2

Handwriting activities from Jelly and Bean

Name.................................. Date..................

Write over the dotted letters and colour the picture.

m m m m
m a t m a t
s a t c a t s

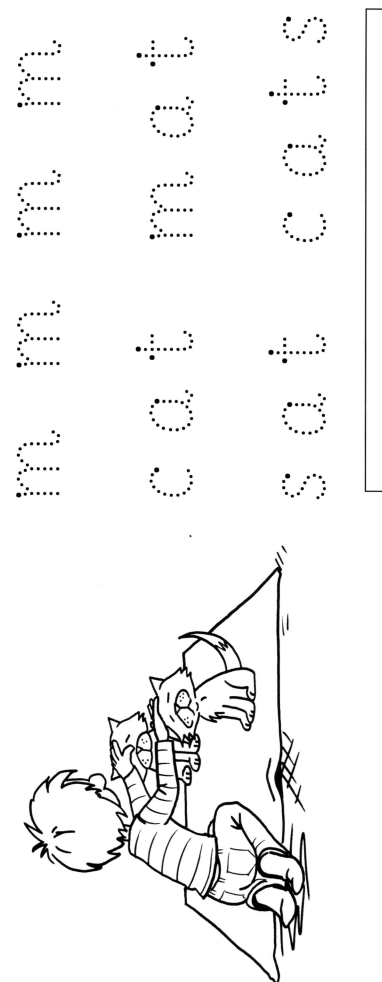

Write the missing letter in each word.

| a | t | m | s |

m _ t   c a _ .....
_ a t   c a _ .....

Book 2 Activity 3   Handwriting activities from Jellly and Bean

Name.. Date..................

Write over the dotted letters and colour the picture.

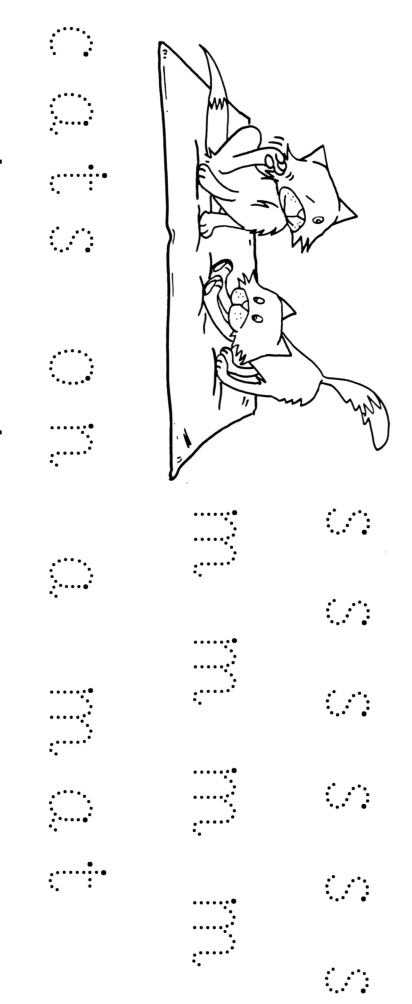

s s s s s s

m m m m m

c a t s   o n   a   m a t

Write **cats on a mat** on the dotted line below.

....

Name.. Date................................

Draw a line from each phrase to the correct picture.
Colour the pictures.

cats on a mat

a mat on cats

cats and a big tin

Name.. Date..................................

Practise writing the letters.

Write the letters o d g by yourself on the dotted line.

Write the letters t i f by yourself on the dotted line.

Name.................... Date....................

Write over the dotted letters and colour Bella.

Bella   Bella   Bella

Write **Bella** on the dotted line by yourself.

....

Book 3 Activity 1

Handwriting activities from Jellly and Bean

Name.. Date....................

Draw a line from each phrase to the correct picture.

| a rabbit on a bed |

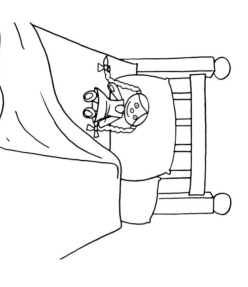

| a doll on a bed |

| Bella in bed |

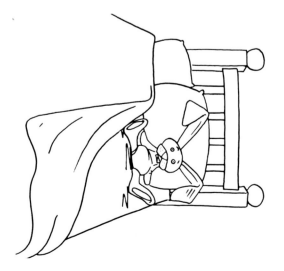

Write the words **a bag on a bed** on the dotted line.

....

Name.................................. Date..................

Write over the dotted letters and colour the picture.

rabbit

rabbit rabbit

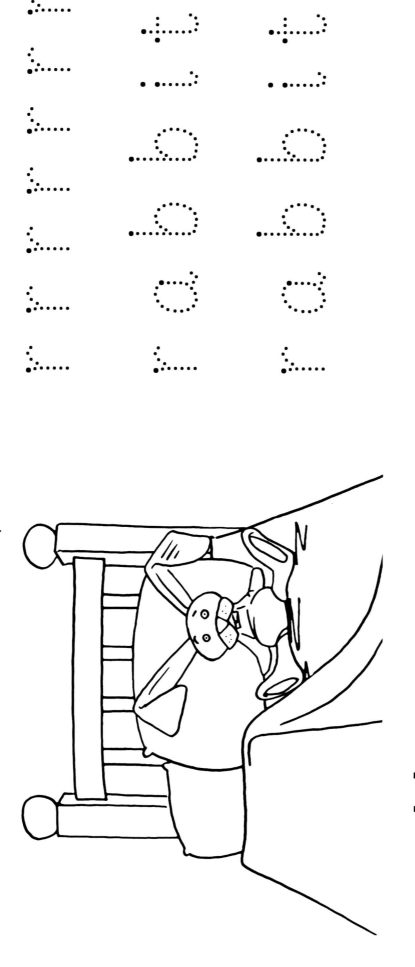

Write **rabbit** on the dotted line by yourself.

....

Name... Date...

Draw a line from each phrase to the correct picture.

| Bella **and** a bag |

| Bella **and** a doll |

| Bella **and** a rabbit |

Write the words **bag doll rabbit** on the dotted line.

....

Book 3 Activity 4

Handwriting activities from Jelly and Bean

Name.................... Date....................

Write over the dotted letters and colour the picture.

e e e e e
bed bed
Bella Bella
Bella Bella

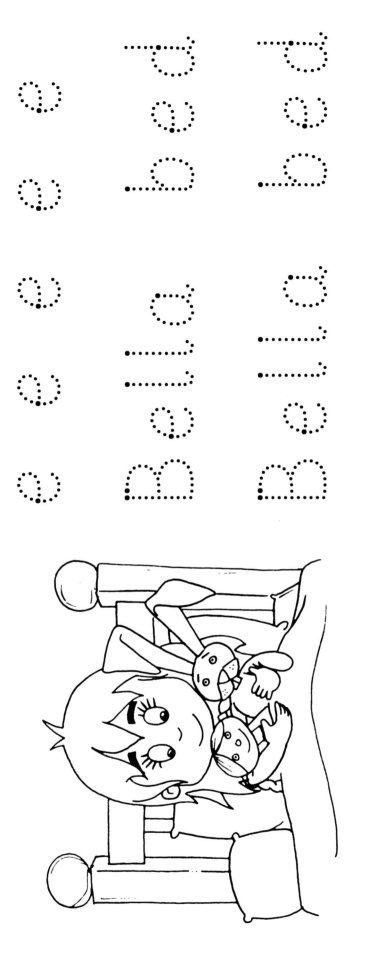

Write the words **Bella in bed** on the dotted line.

....

Book 3 Activity 5   Handwriting activities from Jellly and Bean

Name.. Date..........................

Practise writing the letters.

Write the letters **b** and **d** by yourself on the dotted line as many times as you can.

Book 3 Activity 6

Handwriting activities from Jelly and Bean

Name................................ Date................

Write over the dotted letters. Join each picture to the correct words.

the cats

the dog

the big

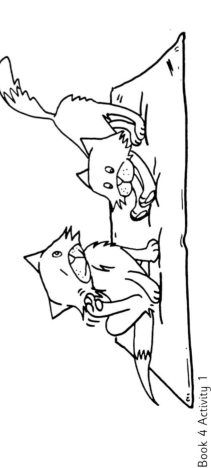

Book 4 Activity 1

Handwriting activities from Jelly and Bean

Name.. Date..................................

Write over the dotted words and colour the picture.

pan   pan

cup   cup

bad   bad

Write the letters **b p d** on the dotted line as many times as you can.

....

Name.................................... Date....................

Draw a line from each phrase to the correct picture.

| the cat on the cups |

| the cat on the pans |

| pans and cups |

Write the words **cups pans** on the dotted line.

....

Book 4 Activity 3   Handwriting activities from Jelly and Bean

Name.. Date..

Write over the dotted letters and join the pictures to the correct words.

| in the bag |
| on the dog |
| in the bin |

in on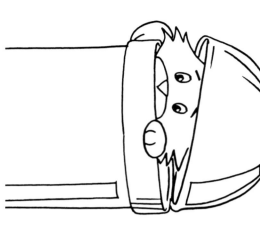

in on

in on

Name... Date.............................

Write over the dotted letters and colour the picture.

the the the

and and and

Write **and** and **the** in the spaces below.

Bella .... bad cat

Book 4 Activity 5

Handwriting activities from Jellly and Bean

Name.. Date..

Write over the dotted letters and colour the picture.

up up up

cup pan

bad cat

Write the missing letter in each word.

u b a p

...an ...ad

...up ...at

Name.................................... Date....................

Write over the dotted letters and colour the picture.

.....bus .....has

.....big .....red

.....bus .....has

Write **has** and **bus** in the spaces below.

.....Tom .....a .....big red..............

Book 5 Activity 1

Handwriting activities from Jelly and Bean

Name.. Date..........................

Write over the dotted letters and colour the pictures.

The big red bus is fast.

Write the letters S and f on the dotted line.

....

Book 5 Activity 2

Handwriting activities from Jelly and Bean

Name.. Date..................................

Write over the dotted letters and colour the pictures.

.....The bus hits the bin.

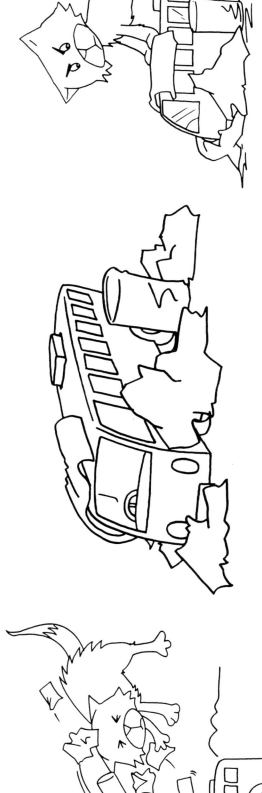

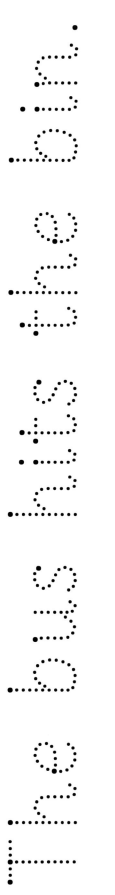

Write the sentence 'The cat is mad.' by yourself on the dotted line.

....

Name.. Date..................

Draw a line from each sentence to the correct picture.

| Tom has a tin. |

| Bella has a cup. |

| Tom has a bus. |

Write the letters b h n m r on the dotted line.

....

Book 5 Activity 4

Handwriting activities from Jellly and Bean

Name................................. Date..................

Draw a line from each sentence to the correct picture.

| Tom is mad. | | The cat is mad. |

| The cat is sad. |

Write the words **bad   mad   sad** on the dotted line.

....

Book 5 Activity 5   Handwriting activities from Jellly and Bean

Name.. Date..........................

Draw a line from each phrase to the correct picture.

| the kitten in the bag |

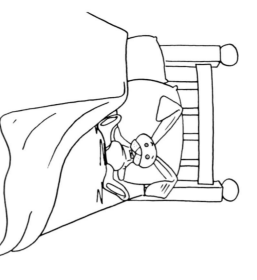

| the rabbit on the bed |

| the button on the bus |

Write the words **rabbit** and **kitten** on the dotted line.

....

Book 5 Activity 6   Handwriting activities from Jelly and Bean

Name............................. Date.............

Write over the dotted letters and colour the pictures.

Bella sat on the mat.

Write the sentence by yourself on the dotted line.

....

Book 6 Activity 1

Handwriting activities from Jellly and Bean

Name.. Date....................................

Draw a line from each sentence to the correct picture.

| The cups drip. |

| Bella fills the cups. |

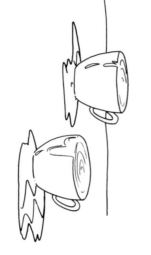

| The pot tips up. |

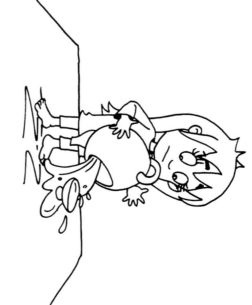

Write the words **cup pot tip** on the dotted line.

....

Name.................................... Date....................

Draw a line from each word to the correct item in the picture.

| mat |
| cup |
| wet |

| mug |
| pot |
| Bella |

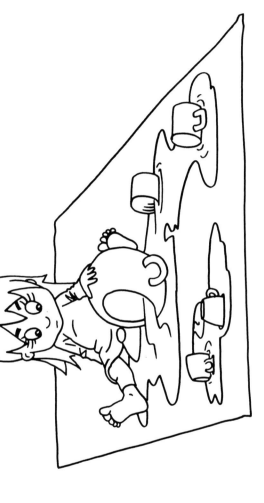

Write each word by yourself on the dotted lines.

....

....

Book 6 Activity 3

Handwriting activities from Jelly and Bean

Name.. Date....................

Draw a line from each sentence to the correct picture.

| The mat is wet. |

| Bella is in bed. |

| Bella is wet. |
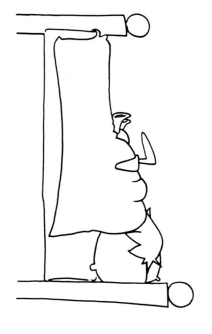

Write the sentence **Bella is in bed** on the dotted line.

....

Book 6 Activity 4 — Handwriting activities from Jelly and Bean

Name.................... Date....................

Write over the dotted letters and colour the picture.

w w w

wet wet

wet wet

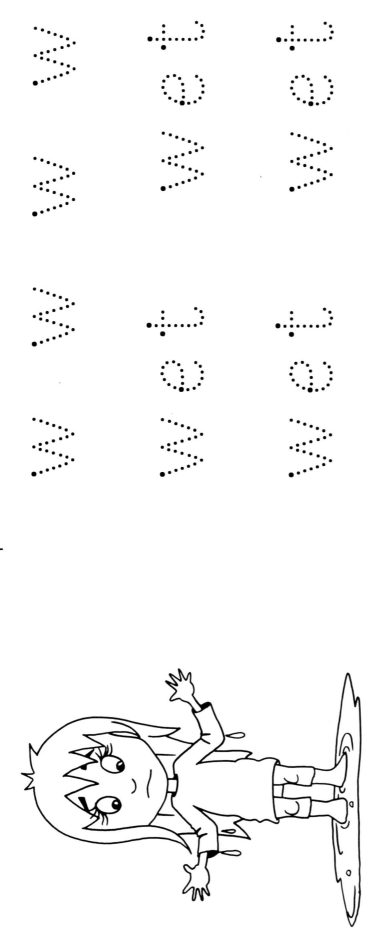

Write **Bella is wet** on the dotted line by yourself.

....

Book 6 Activity 5

Handwriting activities from Jellly and Bean

Name... Date...........................

Write the correct word in each sentence.

| bus | mess | bed |

1 Tom is in ....

2 The cat is on the ....

3 Bella has a .... on the mat.

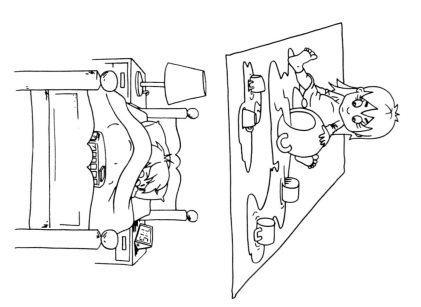
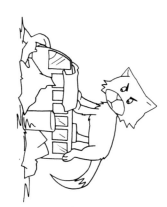